I remember
GORLESTON

by

J. E. Holmes

with Dean Parkin

Jim Holmes

First published 1996 by Rushmere Publishing
32 Rushmere Road, Carlton Colville, Lowestoft, Suffolk

Typeset by Chemtech Graphics
Sussex Road, Gorleston, Great Yarmouth, Norfolk

Printed in England by Blackwell John Buckle
Charles Street, Great Yarmouth, Norfolk NR30 3LA

ISBN 1 872992 11 0

I remember *GORLESTON*

by

J. E. Holmes
with Dean Parkin

ACKNOWLEDGEMENTS

The Gorleston I like to remember is preserved forever in the paintings of the town by A. C. Mellon, which are currently hanging in the James Paget Hospital. However, it is also preserved in my own recollections and those of my friends, who I would like to thank for helping to jog these memories.

Credit must also be given to Christine Johnson for proof-reading, Dean Parkin for all his efforts, and Brooke Bond, not just for their tea but for their permission to use the drawing of the Trojan van. I must thank Ivor Davis too, a true character of Gorleston, for the use of the photograph of himself.

The photographs in this kind of book are always important and with this in mind I would like to give a special word of thanks to Percy Trett, who allowed me access to his superb collection, and whose pictures serve to illustrate this volume.

Introduction

The second time Alan Cobholm and his Flying Circus came to town in 1932 to promote air travel, I was lucky enough to fly in an old First World War Avro fighter over Gorleston and Yarmouth. He didn't seem to create much enthusiasm in Gorleston as I turned out to be the only person waiting for a flight, but the pilot was anxious to arouse interest so he said he would take me up anyway.

It was an ex-RAF pilot by the name of Captain Phillips who strapped me in the rear cockpit and started the engine. It roared into life and with great excitement we were soon bumping along the makeshift airfield, about where the James Paget Hospital is today, to turn into the wind. With full throttle we climbed steadily until land lay way below and then we turned and flew over the sea where I tried to pick out landmarks. Suddenly a great force seemed to be pressing me down in the cockpit and everything was upside down. Then I was pushed up the other way. We'd looped the loop! It had taken my breath away, but when it happened again I was ready and really enjoyed the sensation. I had a marvellous trip, all for five shillings and I was sorry to land!

Looking down from that plane, I saw a Gorleston that was attractive, full of life and interest, well kept everywhere with the beach its pride and joy. My memories of this town mostly cover the years between 1920 and the start of the Second World War. It was during those years that I happily remember staying with my Aunt Edith and my cousins Betty and Joyce during summer holidays at a house near the top of Albemarle Road. Whether it was let for the summer or was a small boarding house I do not recall but I well remember the large scooter which I borrowed from my cousins and rode furiously down the steep pavement towards Lowestoft Road, a danger to myself and everyone else!

Gorleston's seafront circa 1908 with the Pavilion shown in the centre. Opened only a few years previously, in July 1901, it soon established itself as a popular venue for concert parties. It was designed by the then Borough Surveyor, Mr. J. W. Cockrill, but its style seems a little odd and doesn't really match its surroundings.

The Seaside Town

The Seaside Town

When I was a youngster Gorleston was an ideal seaside resort – lovely flat wide sands that gently sloped out from the cliffs to the sea, so much safer and warmer than Yarmouth. Whole families spent their days enjoying the beach and the sea, with costumes available if needed and refreshments close to hand. There were the ever popular 'Punch and Judy' shows near the boating pool, which was a great attraction in itself with all kinds of model boats, some clockwork and some were even model steam driven vessels! The centre of attention was always Captain Mobbs' wonderful scale models of world famous racing yachts like Tommy Lipton's *Shamrock*. Old Captain Mobbs was the chief Trinity House pilot and would arrive at the pool immaculately dressed and every inch a captain. He was friendly, kindly and helpful to young admirers but he particularly favoured me as I believe he knew my grandfather, another well known seafarer.

Beside the beach was the swimming pool which I always found very cold! It was built in 1938 where the bandstand had stood previously but today this area has been returned to its former look, the swimming pool filled in and the site turned into a garden. The Parade was much as it is today but better kept. The cliffs, paths and

---

◀ (Facing page)

Aerial view of Gorleston Beach, 1956, showing how much beach was left before the building of the new pier six years later. In the centre of the photograph you can see the bathing pool and the Ocean Room (then the Floral Hall) which opened together in July 1939. On the left is the boating pool, which was a great attraction itself in its day. Sailing craft of all sorts and sizes were brought along by their young owners, and there were clockwork motor boats and even model steam-driven vessels!

At the top of the photograph can be seen Yarmouth power station still under construction.

Gorleston seafront was still largely undeveloped in the late 1880s, around the time this photograph was taken. With none of the landmarks by which the town can be identified such as the Pier Hotel or the Pavilion, one realises how much the town grew in the short space of time of the late Victorian and early Edwardian period. Indeed, only a small segment of the cliffs have been tamed here, with a path and shelter having been built.

Also, note the masts of the sailing ships on the horizon.

the garden which were bought by the Council in 1928 for £27,000, were all rather formal compared with today but Gorleston was more of a sedate and genteel family resort than old rollicking Yarmouth.

One of the main attractions in Gorleston at this time was the 'Pops'. Henry Clay's Pops were a seaside concert party who performed during the season in a large concert hall on Beach Road. Mr. and Mrs. Clay would always arrive before the rest of the company in their large 'Standard' touring car loaded with big baskets on the carrier and on the back seat and young Henry Clay arrived around the same time in his dashing little Triumph sports car. The whole family took part in the performances. Mrs Clay was a good singer, although a little past her best, while Henry Clay Senior had a very impressive voice, modelling himself on the famous Bransby Williams. The rest of the party included several dancers, funnymen and the usual seaside acts and they all lodged in accommodation nearby. The hall has long since gone but I understand the area is still referred to as 'Pops Meadow' after all these years.

The Pier Hotel was always popular with visitors, sited at the beginning of the pier and later kept by Mr. and Mrs Oakes. With their son and daughter, Ernest and Bibby, they established a great reputation for themselves, attracting many well known personalities as summer visitors. One I remember was Heddle Nash, a famous operatic singer in his day.

A shooting gallery hut was near the harbour-light tower and was owned by 'Whimsical' Walker, one of the real characters of Gorleston. He was a retired circus clown of international fame and very popular, especially with the girls. He wasn't very fond of little boys though – I expect we were too cheeky!

Other well known personalities in Gorleston between the Wars were Ivor Davis and Jasper Matthews. Ivor Davis was a very skilled railway engineer and later a steam engine driver. He was a most versatile engineer and even built his own motor boat, the *Rovi*, his name backwards. Now well over ninety, he still drives his car and regularly attends meeting of the model engineers society and privately attends to small engineering problems. He proudly claims to be one of the first to sit in an aeroplane too. Ivor was present when Bleriot completed his first flight over the Channel and when it had landed the great man sat the young Ivor in the cockpit!

Ivor Davis has seen many changes in a lifetime which spans this century. A very skilled railway engineer and later a steam engine driver, he saw the halcyon days of the railway and the conversion from steam to diesel. In fact he is pictured here, on the far right, at a diesel training course for steam engine drivers.

Gorleston beach and seafront before the First World War, with its 'village' of tents and bathing machines. You could hire tents from any one of a number of family businesses such as Denton's, Dye's or Austrin's, which can all be seen in this photograph.

In 1904 a move to establish a Singers' Ring on Gorleston's beach, similar to the one at Great Yarmouth, met with such protest that the plan was quickly withdrawn.

The seafront from another angle, taken around 1910, showing the standard of dress of the time. On the horizon can be seen a Belle steamer, which can be pinpointed by the steam that it is trailing, heading towards the South Pier.

Belle steamers stopped regularly at Gorleston after 1905 providing a daily service bound for Lowestoft, Southwold, Felixstowe and Walton. These excursions were hugely popular but they didn't always go according to plan as on one particular occasion on August 16th, 1938. Heading for Ostend in Belgium with over a thousand passengers, the Queen of the Channel was caught by a strong tide as she passed Gorleston's South Pier and ploughed into it, cutting through a one foot thick wooden pile and making a twenty-foot breach into the quay. Many passengers were injured and at least eleven required hospital treatment. After twenty minutes the Queen of the Channel was freed from the pier with its bow severely damaged but managed to return to Fish Quay in Great Yarmouth where fares were refunded.

Opened in 1898, the Cliff Hotel was designed by a Norwich architect John Skipper, who designed many other notable hotels on the east coast such as the Sheringham Hotel and the Victoria Hotel on Kirkley Cliff in Lowestoft.

In its short life the hotel became very much part of Gorleston, and on 4th July, 1905 it was the site of the official banquet celebrating the opening of the new electric tramway in the town. The end came on Boxing Day, 1915 when the building was gutted by fire and, ironically, next day the trams had their busiest day of the year, transporting the many thousands who came to see the ruins of the hotel.

Photograph showing the Beach Gardens and Bandstand which were built in 1902. Over the next few years Yarmouth Corporation spent heavily on improving Gorleston, developing away from the old fishing village's narrow streets and concentrating on the cliffs instead. Soon Marine Parade was extended and shelters were built while a ravine was cut through the cliffs making a direct route to the beach, with a picturesque bridge put over it.

In the winter 'Whitey' Capps would store his bathing machines on land to the rear of the lighthouse, as shown in this photograph. Bathing machines were introduced to Gorleston by the Capp's family in the 1890s. You could either have a single machine or a family machine, which was double the width of the single and had two doors. Capp's two sons would even provide the nervous bather with swimming lessons if required!

Jasper Matthews was a local scrap merchant on Beccles Road and because of his work he was grimy and scruffy. He had a deceptively casual easy-going manner but knew the scrap trade from A to Z and was very shrewd. I had several deals with him and always found him very straight and helpful but it was wise buying and selling that was the root of his success. He also had a smashing daughter, a real beauty, the apple of his eye and his pride and joy.

Another well-known character was Mr. Jimmy Saunders who had a greengrocery round which he usually did accompanied by his little son Kenny. Jimmy was often referred to as 'the Mayor of Burgh Castle', being active in local politics but I particularly remember him for his unusual car, which was a Trojan Tourer. These vehicles were quite a feature in the the old days and the Brooke Bond tea company operated a fleet of bright red Trojan vans from depots in Beach Road, Gorleston, in the premises which had been the 'Lousy Quarters' Cinema, and from White Horse Plain in Great Yarmouth. Another memorable sight in the town were the Walls ice cream tricycles with their riders calling out, "Wallsie! Wallsie!" as they rang their cycle bells.

The Brooke Bond tea company had a fleet of bright red vans like the one shown. The vans were very eye-catching and had $2^1/_2$" deep solid tyres and could reach a top speed of 30 m.p.h. With brakes only on their rear wheels, in emergencies the reverse gear could be used for braking without harming the vehicle.

The town centre was always worth a visit and it makes my mouth water whenever I recall Matthes Bakery that used to be on the corner of England's Lane in Gorleston. What a selection of cakes they offered, a penny each or seven for sixpence! One was so full of currants that we named it 'dead flies' but like all the others it was delicious and it was a treat just to look in the shop window. Later they had other shops and extensive van deliveries over a large area, a very fine firm. They also took over Hills the well known Yarmouth restaurant and shop and brought it up to date.

In the 1920s trams ran from Yarmouth bridge to the pier at Gorleston, along Southtown Road, up the High Street, down Baker's Street, Pier Walk, and Brush Quay to the pier. They were originally horse-drawn trams until they switched to electricity and were finally replaced by buses. Though trams caused holdups at times it wasn't too bad as there was not so much traffic in those days.

My favourite cinema in Gorleston was the Coliseum, owned by Mr. Douglas Attree in all his majesty, bow ties and all, a great character who presented many fine films and shows in the old theatre. The cinema certainly broadened our horizons, opening up a new world of of travel, adventure and romance in those hard times of national depression and unemployment. What a choice we had, with great actors like Spencer Tracy, the Barrymore brothers, Lew Stone, Tom Walls, Ralph Lynn, Winifred Shotter, Robertson Hare and so many others. How I dreamed of Janet Gaynor and longed to be like Joel McCrea!

Near the Coliseum in the High Street was Hammond's the ironmongers, now Cooper's, and a hairdresser's called Bridgeman's who cut my hair for fourpence when my thatch was still thick. Now it's scanty and costs a fortune! An interesting little backroad found just off the High Street is Blackwall Reach, where I remember Rudd's the blacksmith's had their premises.

Opposite Woolworth's, on the corner of Church Road was Bernard Bootham the tobacconist who was well known for his Toc H and other activities, while across the road was the tramway depot. Next to that was the *Tramway Hotel*, which was kept by Mr. and Mrs Marjoram who had four sons, George, Herbert and the twins. Sadly during the Second World War the building was bombed and both Mr. and Mrs. Marjoram were killed. The Library stands on the site today.

Gorleston's first cinemas opened within a month of each other. Filmland in Beach Road opened on 21st July 1913 and during its history went through many name changes, being known as The Playhouse, The Palace, Scala and Louis Quatorze, which the locals quickly nicknamed 'Lousy Quarters'! The Coliseum, pictured here around 1950, was built in the High Street on the site of the Fisher's Institute and opened on August Bank Holiday, 1913, with the film, 'Mysteries of Paris'. Later, in 1939, another cinema was opened in the High Street across the road from Mr. Voll's newsagents shop and near the Post Office and Police Station. Known as The Palace, it closed in 1964 to become a bingo hall.

Stead & Simpson had two shops in Gorleston in my youth. In addition to the one shown here at No. 112 High Street with four gas lanterns outside, they also had premises in Bells Road. This photograph was taken around 1910, when alongside Stead & Simpson were the shops belonging to James Albert Bussey, a big grocery and drapery store, which could be found at Nos. 111, 113, 114 and 115.

Situated on the Lowestoft Road and Church Lane corner, Hammond's was one of Gorleston's largest shops in its day, and is shown here just after the turn of the century. Cooper's have the premises now.

Tramway Hotel and Norton's corner, shortly before the Second World War. The hotel was built on the site of the Horse and Groom public house which was demolished in the early 1870s and had tennis courts laid out alongside it in 1921. Sadly, the Tramway met its demise in June 1941 when it was destroyed in an air raid and lives were lost. The hotel was later rebuilt following a temporary building which was put up after the War.

The oldest public house in the town is still *The Feather's Inn* with Feather's Plain being one of the oldest parts of the town. Nearby in the High Street was Platten's clothing and household furnishers, alongside Herbert's the florists, which in its day was the leading florist in the town with their nursery on Burgh Road. From the *Feather's*, it's a short walk over the road into Baker Street where you could find the premises that were later to become Bussey's Stores, which was a grocers. Mr Boulton was the manager and he was also a very popular entertainer with his concert party.

On the corner of England's Lane was Walter English's cycle shop where I had my cycle repaired, and always bought lamps and tyres too. After leaving Matthes we would usually stop and look in the windows of L. & L. Durrant, the gentlemen's outfitters. In my teens much of my outfit was bought there and how cheap everything was in those hard-up times. Flannel trousers cost from 10/6d to 16/-, sports jackets 10/- to £1, singlets 1/- to 1/6d, the popular 'Swallow' raincoats £1 1s 0d and the 'Big Shot' trilby hat, favoured by the film stars, 2/6d each. Mr. Durrant was usually in the shop and was always a nice man to deal with. Louis, his son, was the buyer for the business and made frequent trips to London in his Essex Super Six American saloon car which had terrific acceleration and high speeds even on the narrow winding roads of those days. As you can imagine Louis was quite a dashing figure, and something of a hero to a teenager all those years ago.

Next I remember a small tobacconist shop and then Beaver's fish shop which always had lots of shrimps which they caught offshore. I much admired the blue eyed, flaxen haired girl who usually sold shrimps there, a smashing Viking maiden who never even noticed me! 'Slasher' Watts the barber was the next shop along, he was a jovial little man, full of beans, who also sold saucy postcards in addition to other holiday goods.

Opposite Dr. Anderson's surgery on Pier Plain, near Perfect's Cartage business, was Weaver's dairy. He delivered in a motor-cycle and sidecar, with the milk served from a churn and measured into jugs or other containers. Another independent milkman in the town was Angus Maclellan, a fine looking Scot who married one of the Longs and my word, didn't she rule the roost! In Beach Road there was also a single cow dairy, kept by a Mr. Algar, who would sell milk to anyone bringing jugs

(Right)
An unusual Victorian letter box was part of Bussey's premises, in the High Street until 1959, and is now in the Tolhouse Museum.

(Below)
Bussey's grocery shop in the High Street is pictured after it had closed in 1968 when it had moved to Baker Street. The High Street premises were demolished and a new shopping development erected in its place although the building to the far right is still standing.

or cans to be filled. I doubt if this would be allowed today but regulations were fairly lax in those days. Also in Beach Road was the water pump, which by the late 1930s seemed rather neglected. It was established by Admiral Duncan, the winner of the battle of Camperdown in 1797, when he was stationed with his fleet at Yarmouth and found difficulty in watering his ships. It seems the town water was so bad that he decided to sink a well in Gorleston himself and supply his ships from there!

From Pier Plain we looked over to Bells Marsh Road where we could see the Corporation transport depot, all open land at the Baker Street end. At this time they were mostly horse-drawn flat lorries and tumbrils. I always remember one of their carters named Warnes, standing with the reins in one hand and saluting his friends with the other and a loud, "What cheer, Charlie!" He had gingery whiskers and hair like a halo under a cap set at a jaunty angle. He always wore a brightly coloured neckerchief and corduroy trousers with straps below the knees. Swaying and balancing as he drove at a smart pace in his happy, friendly way he reminded me of Ben Hur. He enjoyed life as it came and I remember him with pleasure as a beam of sunshine!

At the bottom of England's Lane on the corner of Beach Road and Cliff Hill was Brett's popular fish and chip shop where there was always a queue. Three penny pieces of fish and threepenn'th of chips used to feed a family! Nearly opposite, on Pier Walk, was 'Sharky' Rose's eating house, usually filled with summer visitors tucking in to a very good meal for 1/- or 1/6d. I still remember the taste of the lovely steak and kidney puddings, the roast beef with two vegetables and feather light Yorkshire pudding, followed by suet pudding and treacle, apple pie or jam roly poly, to name but a few of the delicious dishes Mrs. Rose so expertly cooked. Sadly, Mrs Rose suffered a personal tragedy when she lost her only son in an accident and never got over it. Sharky Rose was a bit of a character in his time and was always very active in the fishing season supplying groceries to the Scots drifters on the Gorleston side of the river.

Near Sharky were two grocers opposite each other, Andrew's on one side of the road, and Wilson's on the other, adjoining the chapel. One of the lay preachers was 'Trarky' Leak, who lived with his family in Bell's Marsh Road. One of his sons, Archie, later had Leak's Garage on the Quayside. 'Trarky' was a well known figure

Cliff Hill was also known as 'Deadman's Hill' or 'Pilfer Hill' in the nineteenth century at a time when beachmen were having houses built in this area. It was rumoured that the money for these houses was ill-gotten, the result of the murder of a Jewish man whom the beachmen were rowing ashore. The large heavy chest he was carrying was full of gold and rich lace and it was said that the contents were divided equally amongst the crew. Whether this tale is true or a result of jealousy we can't be sure, but it does show that this was a rich era for the beachmen and their salvage work however they acquired their wealth.

in the town and in addition to being a lay preacher and teetotaller, he was also a marine store dealer. One day he was being driven over Yarmouth old bridge in a Model 'T' Ford lorry when the driver pressed the pedal into reverse by mistake and the lorry swerved and shot 'Trarky' into the doorway of a pub at the foot of the bridge. It was said to be the first and only time he entered a public house!

Along the quayside you could find the warehouse, offices and shop of the On-The-Square-Library, which claimed to be the largest twopenny circulating library in East Anglia with 89 branches from Retford to Clacton and Cambridge to Cromer and many agents. That was in the 1930s and the shops were extraordinarily popular, although the business collapsed when the public libraries modernised and expanded.

Bells Road was another shopping area, catering for the other side of Gorleston. I remember there was a large stationer's shop there, known as Spain's and William's haberdashery shop. Nearby in Victoria Road was the Gorleston Garage managed by Tommy Waldron and it certainly was a flourishing business and reputed to be the first garage to have petrol pumps in the area. Victoria Road eventually meets Lowestoft Road and across the railway bridge on the right was Mr. Page's Bee Hive garage from where he operated the Bee Line Buses. They were new Bedford buses and offered real bargains, for example, London for 5/6d or return 8/-! Just past this garage in Lowestoft Road was Gorleston station. The train used to stop at Hopton and then Corton with a special stop for Corton Gardens, a big attraction years ago. From Lowestoft the line ran to Ipswich to join the London train from Norwich. Another line connected with Norwich via Oulton Broad, Somerleyton and Reedham, a lovely trip.

Perhaps one of the finest view points of Gorleston is from the top of Cliff Hill, where you can see the remains of the Cliff Hotel, a typically imposing Victorian building dominating the Front which burnt down on Boxing Day 1915, during a terrible westerly gale. The hotel was thought to be one the finest on the east coast and indeed, the view from its rooms must have made the Victorian and Edwardian holidaymaker feel they were really by the seaside!

The beach in my era, circa 1925. If you look carefully you can see the pier and 'cosies' are lined with people and the promenade is packed! I have happy memories of the beach. Gorleston had lovely sands flat, wide, extending from the cliff and sloping out to sea. People were satisfied just to be there.

The Pier Hotel on the left was built in the early 1890s on the site of the Anchor and Hope public house, which had been a popular venue for boatmen throughout the 1800s.

A horse tram arrives at Feather's Plain in 1886. First proposed in 1870, construction on the three mile horse-drawn tramway in Gorleston began in October 1871 and was completed in the early months of 1875. Opened by the Mayor of Yarmouth, R.D. Barber, and operated by the East Suffolk Tramway Company, the service connected Gorleston with Southtown Station and on its first day its receipts were a princely £20! The service ran at quarter-hourly intervals but it could take two and a half hours to complete the journey on any one of the ten cars originally serving the route.

In April 1878 the Yarmouth and Gorleston Tramways Company was formed and it acquired the original tramway company, bringing urgently needed funds to the business which was losing money due in part to its initial expenditure. The result was that a reconstruction of the tramway took place in 1882 with new rails being laid and a depot and stables were erected at Yarmouth.

Horse tram on Feather's Plain around 1900, about to make the return trip to Yarmouth. At the turn of the century a 'tip' or extra horse was used for pulling trams up the steep incline at the junction of England's Lane and Lowestoft Road.

In the summer ten cars operated the service, reducing to five cars in the autumn until Christmas, after which four cars managed until the summer trade returned. In 1904, the last full year of the horse tramway, 1,193,338 passengers were conveyed paying £6,964 for the privilege.

An electric tram on Lowestoft Road near the Springfield Road terminus. In 1905 the Gorleston horse tramway was bought by the Yarmouth Corporation for £13,211 11s 3d, and the route was electrified providing a much better service for Gorleston's ever expanding reputation as a seaside resort.

Six hundred men were employed immediately to begin work on the electrification of the tramway under the supervision of the Borough Surveyor and in ten weeks a new depot was erected on a site adjacent to the old horse car depot. During the work horse buses, that were no longer used in Yarmouth, took over in places where the tramway was being laid.

On 4th July 1905 the new electric tramway was officially opened. Although the Corporation now ran both the Great Yarmouth and Gorleston trams, the Gorleston section ran almost as a separate undertaking with its own staff, which consisted of a cashier, a clerk, two inspectors and a relief, a foreman, four night cleaners, a day cleaner, a body builder and three car mechanics. Indeed, Great Yarmouth and Gorleston were always to remain unconnected by trams due to the impossibility of laying tracks on the Haven Bridge.

At Feather's Plain the tramway divided, with one route heading for the beach and the other along Lowestoft Road to the railway station.

During the First World War the tramway was scarcely maintained due to a shortage of parts, raw materials and skilled craftsmen. When hostilities ceased, money needed to be spent on repair to the track and the trams themselves had to be ignored. The introduction of three buses in June 1920, bought from the London General Omnibus Company for £1,725, did little to quell the demise of the tramway although all the tram track was renewed between 1924–26 serving only to amass a huge debt on the part of the Corporation.

Pictured here in the late 1920s, an electric tram is shown on Southtown Road. By this time the Corporation had acquired more buses and at the end of the summer season in 1930 it was estimated that a further £30,000 would have to be spent on repairs to the track and cars of the Corporation's two remaining tramways, Southtown to Gorleston and in Yarmouth, Wellington Pier to Caister. With the success of the new motorised buses, there was little option but to scrap the trams and the Gorleston system closed on 25th September 1930 although the Wellington Pier tramway continued until 1933.

Church Lane pictured in 1890. Among the occupants here at this time were Robert Porter, stone, marble and monumental mason, Nathaniel Woods, who was a bricklayer by trade, John Farman, fish hawker and George Harvey who was a market gardener. Gorleston was certainly a growing town at this time, with the population estimated at around 11,000, having been 9,008 in 1881. Indeed, at the start of the nineteenth century the town had just 1,723 inhabitants.

St. Andrew's Church probably dates from the thirteenth century. An imposing edifice, the church has six bays, long north and south aisles extending the whole length of the church and a western tower. Some ninety feet in height, this tower was a valuable watch tower, for which purpose it was used during the days that Napoleon was shattering the peace of Gorleston. The Church was badly damaged in the reformation when the holy water stoups were demolished along with the stone crosses and numerous stained glass windows while '20 brazen superstitious inscriptions' from the chancel were removed.

The first Christian church to be raised in Gorleston is thought to have come into being in the 7th Century, when St. Felix, the missionary who became Bishop of Dunwich, erected an edifice of wood which fell victim to the mauraudíng Danes two centuries later. However, soon they too were converted to the faith and a new house of worship was constructed of flint and stone. This was probably built on the site of the old wooden one but it is certain that the present St. Andrew's Church was built on the foundation of the Anglo-Saxon building.

During the winter of 1922/23 a new and important road was constructed to link Gorleston church with the Lowestoft Road at Elmhurst, namely Middleton Road. Ten years later a roundabout, the first to be built in the Borough, was made at the Church Lane junction. With the construction of this road Gorleston began to spread westwards and in 1932 the Corporation purchased 958 acres of land from Magdalen College, Oxford for £35,000 which was eventually developed as the Magdalen Estate.

Norton's Corner with its horse chestnut trees before re-construction in 1971. In the background can be seen the tram depot which was erected at Feather's Plain beside the old one and these buildings remained, largely unused, until they were demolished to make way for the new Library which opened on the site in 1974.

The United Service paddle tug is shown leaving the harbour on the right, while another white funnel tug is returning to port with a trawler in tow. This photograph could well have been staged to include the photographer on the left, to show him busy at his work and help publicise his business.

The Maritime Town

The Maritime Town

The popular Old Dutch Pier was so-called in memory of the great Dutch engineer, Joas Johnson, whose advice was sought for a solution to Yarmouth's constantly shifting harbour entrance. Johnson selected the site of Gorleston's present harbour entrance and work began in 1650 on building the remarkable wooden pier which solved the centuries old problem of achieving a stable harbour entrance. In the 1950s the north pier was reconstructed and in 1962 work began on replacing the Old Dutch Pier as well. However, as the 400 year old timbers were removed, the modern engineers failed to see the wisdom of the original design or take into account the flow of the tide and the result was disastrous. The shape of the famous bend was altered and Gorleston lost its beach.

The 'cosies' were a favourite spot for locals and tourists alike. These were the sunny, sheltered areas between the timbers on the south side of the old pier, where people enjoyed themselves for hours watching all the many kinds of vessels that one could see in the harbour in those days. It was an ideal place for line fishing too and the perfect vantage point to see the staged rescues and demonstrations by the local lifeboat, which were put on at the height of the holiday season. The cosies were also the scene of blossoming romance for generations of courting couples!

At the end of this pier was the Coastguard lookout while spaced at intervals were the old capstans used mainly before the advent of steam tugs to draw sailing vessels

---

◀ (Facing page)
A bird's eye view of Gorleston, with the old south pier at the forefront of the picture. In the centre of the picture, beyond the Spending Beach, there can be seen the herring reduction plant built in 1946 to turn the surplus herrings into fish meal. However, fishing was already in decline by then and the plant became defunct.

Two views of the popular 'cosies'. People would spend the whole day here and not just in high summer. Some would fish, some would simply watch the assortment of vessels, or there might be a demonstration with the lifeboat staging a rescue.

The capstans on the Old Dutch Pier, here shown around 1870. As a sailing ship came in with the wind and tide against it they threw the rope ashore and attached it to the capstan and then threaded a long bar through and pushed, with the slats on the ground there to help their feet grip.

into harbour when the wind, tide or mishap prevented their entry. Near the Pier Hotel, at the beginning of the pier, was the Pilot House with its look-out and pilots on duty-watch ready to bring ships into harbour when required. High winds, strong tides and the narrow entrance, in addition to the tricky 'bend', certainly made things difficult at times around Brush Quay and any assistance was more than welcome. The pilot boat was always alongside the pier, ready to take the pilots out to ships requiring their services. Bert Beavers was coxswain of this wonderfully seaworthy boat built by Brookes of Oulton Broad. It had a small cabin forward in which the pilot managed to keep dry but otherwise it was an open cockpit with no shelter for the coxswain.

Bert Beavers was a great character and came from a long line of seafarers, real sailors, hardy, skilful, daring and brave beyond belief. It was a great experience to watch Bert handling the pilot boat in very rough seas crossing the harbour bar at Yarmouth, an expert in his natural element. Some years later he became well known as coxswain of the Gorleston lifeboat. His father was old Albert Beavers, whom I remember as a self-reliant tough old character, lean, wiry, very active, and light on his feet like a cat. To me he looked just as I imagined a pirate would look, with fierce eyes that looked through you, bushy whiskers and a battered old hat, much like the fictional Captain Kettle. At the time I knew him, he still did a bit of shrimping in the *Sophia*, reputed to be one of the oldest shrimpers out of Yarmouth. The engine was either a Handy Billy or an equally ancient Kelvin, so old that no parts were obtainable and Billy Ireson, a well known marine engineer and expert with shrimp boats, used to make the parts as required. These old marine engines used to start on petrol then when hot turn over to paraffin. The Government gave a rebate on the petrol used and fishermen took care to keep the receipts safe and handy.

The length of quay from the lifeboat sheds to the South Pier is known as Brush Quay, taking its name from the Brush Bend where the river was diverted at right angles to form the harbour's mouth. Alongside the quay is Gorleston's lighthouse, built in 1887, and the Storm Company's headquarters where you could usually find Billy Fleming, one of its members, in his rowing boat waiting to take anyone over to Spending beach or to take a rope from any ships needing assistance. Between the Wars the old Beach Companies had almost dwindled away, and Billy was one of the

Three beach companies emerged in the town in the late 1820s and were known as the Storm, the Ranger and the Young Flies Companies. Pictured here around 1890 are some Gorleston boatmen while behind them is the lighthouse, alongside the lookout of the Ranger's Company. In the background by the William the Fourth public house is the look out of the Young Flies Company.

Gorleston's Volunteer Lifeboat Elizabeth Simpson in the 1890s. Probably the most famous of Gorleston's lifeboats, she served from 1888 until 1939 and during that time never once capsized or lost any of her crew.

last surviving members of the Storm Company but was more famous for his role as coxswain of the Gorleston RNLI lifeboat, for which he was awarded medals for gallant service. In his time Billy was Coxswain of the *John and Mary Meilkham* which was stationed at Gorleston from 1924–39 and was launched 155 times and saved 211 lives. It was an open decked lifeboat with no protection for her crew except a canvas dodger and the engine housing. This gave slight protection to the engineer and as many crew as could crouch behind it but not the coxswain, and it is hard for any landsman to appreciate the conditions these men had to put up with. Cold and wet, they were thrown about wildly on a raging sea for many hours at a time.

The lifeboat shed and slips were always interesting and when the maroons went off were very exciting too. All the lifeboatmen came running, seizing their oilies and lifejackets and scrambling onto the boat. The engine would be running with its throaty roar and then the retaining pin was knocked out and the slip doors opened and down the boat rushed with a great splash into the river and away to sea with Coxswain Fleming at the wheel, Beau Darby as engineer, Joe Johnson the bowman and Ellery Harris, Nelson Monson, Shoots Parker and a Beaver or two amongst the rest of the crew. Bowman Johnson was a big built man just right for this job. With his wife he kept the *Riverside Tavern* on the quay just past the lifeboat shed and though it was bombed during the War, I believe they were fortunately not home at that time.

Also on Brush Quay was the Volunteer Lifeboat Shed, home for many years to the *Elizabeth Simpson*, a former sailing and rowing lifeboat built by the famous Beeching Bros. and converted to a motor lifeboat. She had a wonderful record for life saving and was really the last of the famous Beach Company boats. She was presented to the town by Miss Elizabeth Simpson Stone of Norwich and was manned by the Rangers Beach Company, serving at Gorleston from 1888 to 1939, and in that time never once capsized or lost any of her crew, launching 119 times and saving 441 lives. Young George Mobbs was her volunteer engineer (he later became Coxswain of the RNLI lifeboat), and Walter Austrin, Paul Willament and others formed the crew. In emergencies she would still launch, while in the summer she gave sea trips to raise funds for her maintenance which she continued to do until recently.

Further down was a brick building where the Marjoram fleet of speedboats were kept in the winter. These were very fast sea boats seating about eight passengers and running out of the harbour, along the beach and back in again. There were often very choppy seas and it was really thrilling. The young men piloting those craft were real dare-devils performing manoeuvres and taking risks in fairly rough weather which provoked much criticism from the older, more traditional boatmen. No doubt there was a certain amount of jealousy over the popularity of these new fangled craft!

Alongside the *William IV* public house, we come to the landing steps where the river steamers picked up and set down passengers to and from the Town Hall quay at Yarmouth. It was an interesting trip with the variety of vessels in the river in those days. On one trip it wouldn't be unusual to see sailing ships, steam ships, herring drifters, Thames barges or even lightships. Visitors found it fascinating and it was always a popular excursion.

Old Captain Donaldson lived nearby in Pavilion Road. He was a retired Trinity pilot referred to as a 'mud' pilot as he occasionally berthed vessels within the harbour. He was a splendid old Scot and I always liked him because he was so jolly and hearty.

Brush Quay was also home to the harbour tugs *George Jewson* and *Tactful*. The *Jewson* belonged to the Port and Haven Commissioners and the *Tactful* to the Steam Navigation Company. 'Shiner' Collins was skipper of the *George Jewson* and he reckoned she was overloaded after they fitted fire pumps. He claimed she didn't have enough freeboard, was too low in the water and he wasn't happy in her in bad weather. He'd been a drifter skipper and after two mishaps at sea said, "Any more and I pack up". When his boat ran aground in bad weather near the North Pier, true to his word, that was the end for Shiner. Harry Riches, the skipper of the *Tactful*, was another hardy tough old character in the real tug boat tradition and knew the sandbanks and channels like the back of his hand. The *Tactful*, unlike the *Jewson*, had no wheelhouse, only an open bridge protected by a canvas dodger and the skipper at the wheel faced the worst of the elements until safely back in port. Old Harry put to sea whenever humanly possible. The *Tactful* was a fine little sea-going tug and he knew how to handle her.

River steamers undergoing their annual overhaul in the Fellow's Dock at Great Yarmouth in 1953. This photograph shows the different kind of steamers with a single-decked vessel in front and a double-decked one behind.

These river steamers would pick up passengers from the Town Hall in Great Yarmouth and make the short but enjoyable journey to the Brush Quay in Gorleston. The steamers were double-ended and drove either way with propellors and steering gear at both ends. To return, the skipper just moved to the opposite end and off she went.

On the right of the photograph can be seen The Brit, a vessel used for sea trips from the Town Hall to Britannia Pier.

The white-funnelled paddle tug, Tom Perry, which was owned by Nicholson's Towage Company, returning to harbour with Scottish herring luggers in tow. This paddle tug was built at South Shields in 1879 where she ultimately ended her days, being sold back on 30th April 1907. In 1920 she was broken up.

When I was a teenager, further along the quay lay the two large Dutch ocean-going salvage tugs, *Nordzee* and *Oostzee,* fine modern vessels capable of going anywhere in the world if required. I went aboard and the Captain showed me the powerful wireless and other equipment, all very exciting to an impressionable youngster! My friendly host also pressed a large cigar and a big glass of the best Dutch gin on me and I felt very grown up until nearly home when the world began to swim around and the cigar made me sick!

Part of the end of the quayside was known as Mission Quay. The Royal National Mission to Deep Sea Fishermen had their depot and store there, founded in 1881 to combat the growing sale of drink at sea to fishermen by the Dutch coopers who tempted them with cheap tobacco, rum and brandy. At the quay lay their two fine ships, the sailing smack *Sir William Archibald* (LO 401), a London registration, and the steam trawler *Sir Edward P. Wills,* named in recognition of the great support given by the Wills tobacco company. The ships did not fish but were converted to give medical assistance, care, recreation and other services to fishermen and were much appreciated by all engaged in the dangerous and demanding life at sea. It was from here that Wilfred Grenfell went on to establish his great mission to the fishermen of the great banks off Newfoundland.

In the same area was Newman Bros. engineering works. Alec Newman was a typical naval officer, breezy but full of fun, a good engineer and also an enthusiastic member of many local societies. This was a time of economic depression and slump, work was hard to find and money was short. Much of Newman's machinery was old but by making and mending with great ingenuity the difficulties were tackled in true Navy style. With a small permanent staff, they trained many apprentices and, generally speaking, did a remarkable job of work.

Just past Newman's was Percy Darby's, the marine store dealer. His store was an Aladdin's cave, stacked with all manner of bits and pieces from the many vessels he'd broken up, frequently as a result of the collapse of the herring industry. Many of the wooden drifters he bought for a song and stripped them out at the 'dolphins' (mooring stages) opposite his store. All the metal he recovered was unfortunately shipped to Germany which was rapidly re-arming at that time while the bare hulls he floated down to the Spending Beach and broke them up. In many case the timbers were still sound and readily sold for building and other purposes. Many boats were in excellent condition and fit for the sea. Had the owners only been able to hang on to them until the War they would have been really valuable. In his store were many steering wheels, binnacles, ships' bells, compasses, voice pipes and much more that today would fetch a fortune from collectors and restorers.

Further on the cliff side, opposite the Hard was Albert Darby's boat building shed. He specialised in small craft, dingies and rowboats, which were all so well-made and although reasonably priced, unfortunately beyond my pocket at that time. He also repaired craft drawn up on the Hard. The Darby's have long been active on the riverside at Gorleston hence the name Darby's Hard, a sandy sloping beach where boats beached at high water to allow work to proceed as the tide fell.

Next we came to the ferry, a rowing ferry as I recall it, which charged the large numbers crossing to work and back ½d or 1d. It certainly was a difficult and dangerous trip in the busy fishing season! Proceeding onwards, we pass Watney, Coome and Reid's large maltings and reach the gasworks on Southtown Road. The big gasometers were most impressive but the manager's house on the other side of the road was destroyed by a bomb during the War. Many people must remember fetching a huge sack of coke for 1/- to take home on a bicycle or handcart.

Turning back to Gorleston we pass the *Halfway House* public house, now replaced by flats, and move up High Road passing J. A. N. Smith's butcher's shop and, opposite that, Ferryside, the former home of the well known Dr. Henry Wylls who lived there in great style and even had his own coachman! At the junction of High Road and Ferry Hill was the *Barking Smack* public house, reminding us of the Hewitt's Short Blue fleet of trawlers. Not far from here is the Tower House, where the owners or managers of the Short Blue Fleet watched their trawlers returning.

Opposite the lifeboat shed were the gutting troughs and pickling plot of D. Waters and Son, herring curers from Wick in the far north of Scotland. Every year they would come down for the autumn herring fishing and they would usually make the journey in the firm's Chevrolet platform lorry piled high with luggage. Hughie Green was the driver, Don Waters and his yard men John and Eric were passengers, three squeezed into the cab and one sitting on the load. The journey took three days which was very good considering the condition of the roads all those years ago.

The old ferry which took you across to South Quay near the Fish Wharf, with the drifter fleet laid up behind it. In pre-war days it cost a half-penny to cross in the ferry boat and today motorised ferries have replaced these row boats.

The Tower House in the High street, from which the owners or managers of Hewett's Short Blue Fleet could watch their trawlers returning. Now the view is blocked by factories and the sea can't be seen!

LO.93
LO93

◀ (Facing page)

The fleet leaving port around the turn of the century. It was around 1854 that the fishing side of Hewett's business was gradually transferred from Barking to Gorleston, a port nearer to the fishing grounds and now having a rail link with London. The effect of this to the town was enormous, with construction of a variety of buildings such as a large block of premises built on the western side of the harbour, dry docks, engineering works, ice-houses, sail lofts, shipwrights' and carpenters' shops and stores. A big local industry was suddenly booming, employing hundreds of men such as blacksmiths, painters, sail-makers and many others. Gorleston hospital was even established by Hewett's manager, Mr. Harvey-George, for the benefit of the crews. In the latter half of the nineteenth century Hewett's were at the very heart of Gorleston life.

At their peak in the 1880s, Hewett's Short Blue Fleet had 170 trawlers crewed by 2,000 men. The enormity of fishing at this time cannot be underestimated when you consider that from the 1850s to the end of the century, it was estimated that up to twelve thousand men were constantly afloat under sail in various fleets trawling the North Sea.

◀ (Facing page)

The smack Ada (LO93) was owned by Hewett's and is shown here in the 1890s. By the end of this decade the Short Blue Fleet was in severe financial trouble due to the advent of the steam trawler and the decline began with hundreds of men being forced to find work in steam trawlers sailing from other ports. More problems lay ahead when an explosion tore through the company's engineering works which was not fully covered by insurance. Fish prices were low at this time too and in 1901 the end came, the admirals flag was hauled down for the last time and the smacks were laid up. It was said that the huge fleet of smacks lay moored at Gorleston quay for a year or so before many were broken up, some were sold and a few were converted into ketches for the coasting trade. With almost 4,000 people relying on Hewett's for work and housing, Gorleston was devastated.

A few days later the Scots fisher girls would arrive by train at Beach station and Hughie Green would fetch them and their boxes and convey them on the lorry to their lodgings on Cliff Hill or elsewhere. Accommodating them presented obvious difficulties with all the fish scales and smell but landladies were well prepared and they all fitted in somewhere. The 'girls' were of all ages and most had followed the herring all their lives and were experts in their calling, gutting and packing at unbelievable speed in all weathers. Whilst waiting for the fish, out would come their knitting and without using patterns or even looking at the work they could produce Fair Isle or designs of their own. At other times they would link arms and gaily promenade the roads singing Gaelic songs of the islands and highlands and other songs. If they were sad and tired they often turned to hymn singing which could be very moving at times. They were far from home, poorly paid and often overworked. Some married local men and left the fishing.

There were yards all along the quay, Duncan's, Duthie's, Irvine's and others that became disused as fishing went into decline. A few years ago when on holiday in Scotland we visited Wick intending to look up some old friends and learned that D. Waters and Son's yard had been bombed and destroyed in 1940, Don Waters was killed and Hughie Green had died shortly before my visit.

A well known figure on the quayside in the old days was Mr. Rivett, the berthing master. Berthing had to be strictly controlled especially during the busy fishing season and if one boat came alongside the quay in the wrong place, up would come Mr. Rivett on his bicycle and bawl, "You can't lay there!" and after much swearing and argument the vessel was usually moved. Soon Mr. Rivett's call became quite a catch phrase amongst us youngsters so when anyone we knew left a cycle, car or handcart against the wall or kerb we used to yell, "You can't lay there!" as loud as we could!

Until the early 1930s there were about a dozen fish-curing firms in Gorleston and here is one on Dock Tavern Lane with the smiling fisher girls packing barrels. In crews of three they worked non-stop, gutting and packing herrings until all the work was done. They bound their fingers with thick bandages to protect them against knife-cuts and the salt which burned into their wet hands. These bandages, known as 'clooties', were tied with fingers and teeth and washed every night and pegged out to dry.

Scots fisher girls in the High Street, 1901. The 'girls' were of all ages and their arrival in the town was described by the 'Gorleston Times' in September, 1903, "It is interesting to see the newly arrived Scotch specials disgorging their squadrons of red-haired, ruddy-cheeked passengers with countenances of innocence and wonder . . . . Their faces are aglow with health, their hair, innocent of covering, neatly and fashionably done, and with good warm clothing in strong contrast to the shoddy dress of their southern sisters, they present the very embodiment of strength and comeliness. They are happy too, despite their arduous, unpleasant work – ever singing and busily knitting as they take their walks . . . ."

The pickling plot between Pier Plain and Bells Marsh Road. Standing on a muddy mixture of stones, mud, fish scales and herring guts, unprotected from the weather, the 'girls' would gut twenty thousand herrings in a long day. The Scots were keen church-goers and work on Sunday was frowned upon. Having one day in seven also gave the herrings a chance to regroup too.

Today this particular pickling plot is the site of a housing estate.

Crowds were even attracted to the promenade in the most harsh weather, as shown here in 1920.

The quay heading in a storm-lashed state in 1958 before the flood wall was erected. Gorleston had been subject to periodic flooding throughout its history but that certainly didn't prepare it for the notorious east coast floods in 1953, when overflowing water from the River Yare rapidly submerged the quayside. Such was the force of the water that night that the coast watcher in the lantern house was said to have felt the pier sway under his feet as it was being pounded with waves! Indeed, the strength of the water was not to be underestimated and the next day when it had subsided it left behind a scene of devastation with concrete slabs ripped up, iron railings bent and twisted, while benches and assorted debris lay scattered over the scene.

Many of the craft that were seen around Gorleston harbour could be easily identified by the patchwork of their sails. Here we see the sailing smack Duchess, owned by S. Bones of Gorleston, leaving the harbour on a languid tide circa 1890.

The end of the Old Dutch Pier. In 1962 the structure was pulled to pieces after nearly 400 years of service to the town. Its successor, completed in February 1964 has been criticised.

Aerial view from 1963 with the new pier nearing completion. (Overleaf) ▶